Fish & Seafood

Because of the cooking times for the fish, these dishes are very quick and easy to put together – and very tasty too!

Poultry

Chicken and duck really come alive with Chinese cooking. Served with noodles or rice, they also make a really filling meal.

Meat

Chinese cooking techniques work extremely well with beef and pork, with the short cooking times making the meat tender and beautifully spiced.

FLAME TREE RECIPE BOOKS

FLAME TREE has been creating family-friendly, classic and beginner recipes for our bestselling cookbooks for over 12 years now. Our mission is to offer you a wide range of expert-tested dishes, while providing clear images of the final dish so that you can match it to your own results. We hope you enjoy this super selection of recipes – there are plenty more to try! Titles in this series include:

Cupcakes • Slow Cooker • Curries
Chinese • Soups • Baking Breads
Cakes • Simple Suppers • Pasta
Chicken • Fish & Seafood • Chocolate

For more information please visit:
www.flametreepublishing.com

Steamed Monkfish with Chilli & Ginger

INGREDIENTS

Serves 4

700 g/1½ lb skinless monkfish tail
1–2 red chillies
4 cm/1½ inch piece fresh
   root ginger
1 tsp sesame oil
4 spring onions, trimmed and
   thinly sliced diagonally
2 tbsp soy sauce
2 tbsp Chinese rice wine or dry sherry
freshly steamed rice, to serve

To garnish:
sprigs of fresh coriander
lime wedges

1 Place the monkfish on a chopping board. Using a sharp knife, cut down each side of the central bone and remove. Cut the fish into 2.5cm/1 inch pieces and reserve.

2 Make a slit down the side of each chilli, remove and discard the seeds and the membrane, then slice thinly. Peel the ginger and either chop finely or grate.

3 Brush a large heatproof plate with the sesame oil and arrange the monkfish pieces in one layer on the plate. Sprinkle over the spring onions and pour over the soy sauce and Chinese rice wine or sherry.

4 Place a wire rack or inverted ramekin in a large wok. Pour in enough water to come about 2.5 cm/1 inch up the side of the wok and bring to the boil over a high heat.

5 Fold a long piece of tinfoil lengthways to about 5–7.5 cm/2–3 inches wide and lay it over the rack or ramekin. It must extend beyond the plate edge when it is placed in the wok.

6 Place the plate with the monkfish on the rack or ramekin and cover tightly. Steam over a medium-low heat for 5 minutes, or until the fish is tender and opaque. Using the tinfoil as a hammock, lift out the plate. Garnish with sprigs of coriander and lime wedges and serve immediately with steamed rice.

Szechuan Chilli Prawns

INGREDIENTS

Serves 4

450 g/1 lb raw tiger prawns
2 tbsp groundnut oil
1 onion, peeled and sliced
1 red pepper, deseeded and
  cut into strips
1 small red chilli, deseeded
  and thinly sliced
2 garlic cloves, peeled and
  finely chopped
2–3 spring onions, trimmed
  and diagonally sliced
freshly cooked rice or noodles,
  to serve
sprigs of fresh coriander
  or chilli flowers, to garnish

For the chilli sauce:

1 tbsp cornflour
4 tbsp cold fish stock or water
2 tbsp soy sauce
2 tbsp sweet or hot chilli sauce,
  or to taste
2 tsp soft light brown sugar

1 Peel the prawns, leaving the tails attached if you like. Using a sharp knife, remove the black vein along the back of the prawns. Rinse and pat dry with absorbent kitchen paper.

2 Heat a wok or large frying pan, add the oil and, when hot, add the onion, pepper and chilli and stir-fry for 4–5 minutes, or until the vegetables are tender but retain a bite. Stir in the garlic and cook for 30 seconds. Using a slotted spoon, transfer to a plate and reserve.

3 Add the prawns to the wok and stir-fry for 1–2 minutes, or until they turn pink and opaque.

4 Blend all the chilli sauce ingredients together in a bowl or jug, then stir into the prawns. Add the reserved vegetables and bring to the boil, stirring constantly. Cook for 1–2 minutes, or until the sauce is thickened and the prawns and vegetables are well coated.

5 Stir in the spring onions, tip on to a warmed platter and garnish with chilli flowers or coriander sprigs. Serve immediately with freshly cooked rice or noodles.

1

3

4

Sweet-&-Sour Fish with Crispy Noodles

INGREDIENTS

Serves 4

350 g/12 oz plaice fillets, skinned
3 tbsp plain flour
pinch of Chinese five spice powder
2.5 cm/1 inch piece fresh root ginger,
  peeled and grated
4 spring onions, trimmed and
  finely sliced
3 tbsp dry sherry
1 tbsp dark soy sauce
2 tsp soft light brown sugar
1 tsp rice or sherry vinegar
1 tsp chilli sauce
salt and freshly ground black pepper
125 g/4 oz thin, transparent rice
  noodles or rice sticks
oil for deep frying

To garnish:

spring onion tassels
slices of red chilli

FOOD FACT

Chinese five spice powder adds a taste not unlike liquorice to dishes like this. Add just a tiny pinch, as it has a powerful flavour (see p20).

1 Cut the plaice fillets into 5 cm/2 inch slices. Mix the flour with the five spice powder in a bowl. Add the fish, a few pieces at a time, and toss to coat thoroughly. Reserve.

2 Place the ginger, spring onions, sherry, soy sauce, sugar, vinegar and chilli sauce in a small saucepan and season lightly with salt and pepper. Heat gently until the sugar has dissolved, then bubble the sauce for 2–3 minutes.

3 Break the noodles into pieces about 7.5 cm/3 inch long. Heat the oil in a deep fryer to 180°C/350°F. Deep-fry small handfuls of noodles for about 30 seconds, until puffed up and crisp. Remove and drain on absorbent kitchen paper.

4 Deep-fry the plaice for 1–2 minutes, or until firm and cooked. Remove and drain on absorbent kitchen paper.

5 Place the cooked fish in a warmed serving bowl, drizzle over the sauce and garnish with spring onion tassels and slices of red chilli. Pile the noodles into another bowl and serve.

2

3

4

Sweet-&-Sour Prawns with Noodles

INGREDIENTS

Serves 4

425 g can pineapple pieces in
   natural juice
1 green pepper, deseeded and cut
   into quarters
1 tbsp groundnut oil
1 onion, cut into thin wedges
3 tbsp soft brown sugar
150 ml/¼ pint chicken stock
4 tbsp wine vinegar
1 tbsp tomato purée
1 tbsp light soy sauce
1 tbsp cornflour
350 g/12 oz raw tiger prawns, peeled
225 g/8 oz pak choi, shredded
350 g/12 oz medium egg noodles
coriander leaves, to garnish

HELPFUL HINT

This dish works well with Thai jasmine steamed rice and also wholewheat noodles which have a more nutritional value. When using raw tiger prawns, make sure that the black vein that runs along their backs has been completely removed.

1   Make the sauce by draining the pineapple and reserving 2 tablespoons of the juice.

2   Remove the membrane from the quartered peppers and cut into thin strips.

3   Heat the oil in a saucepan. Add the onion and pepper and cook for about 4 minutes or until the onion has softened.

4   Add the pineapple, sugar, stock, vinegar, tomato purée and soy sauce.

5   Bring the sauce to the boil and simmer for about 4 minutes. Blend the cornflour with the reserved pineapple juice and stir into the pan, stirring until thickened.

6   Clean the prawns if needed. Wash the pak choi thoroughly, then shred.

7   Add the prawns and pak choi to the sauce. Simmer gently for 3 minutes or until the prawns are cooked and have turned pink.

8   Cook the noodles in boiling water for 4–5 minutes until just tender.

9   Drain and arrange the noodles on a warmed plate and pour over the sweet-and-sour prawns. Garnish with coriander leaves and serve immediately.

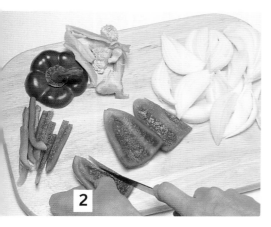

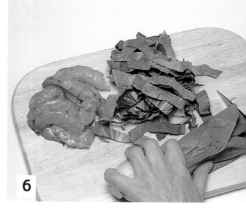

Steamed Whole Trout with Ginger & Spring Onion

INGREDIENTS

Serves 4

2 x 450–700 g/1–1½ lb whole trout,
 gutted with heads removed

coarse sea salt

2 tbsp groundnut oil

½ tbsp soy sauce

1 tbsp sesame oil

2 garlic cloves, peeled and
 thinly sliced

2.5 cm/1 inch piece fresh root ginger,
 peeled and thinly slivered

2 spring onions, trimmed and thinly
 sliced diagonally

To garnish:

chive leaves

lemon slices

To serve:

freshly cooked rice

Oriental salad, to serve

FOOD FACT

There are three types of trout: rainbow, golden and brown, with rainbow trout being the most widely available.

1 Wipe the fish inside and out with absorbent kitchen paper then rub with salt inside and out and leave for about 20 minutes. Pat dry with absorbent kitchen paper.

2 Set a steamer rack or inverted ramekin in a large wok and pour in enough water to come about 5 cm/2 inches up the side of the wok. Bring to the boil.

3 Brush a heatproof dinner plate with a little of the groundnut oil and place the fish on the plate with the tails pointing in opposite directions. Place the plate on the rack, cover tightly and simmer over a medium heat for 10–12 minutes, or until tender and the flesh is opaque near the bone.

4 Carefully transfer the plate to a heatproof surface. Sprinkle with the soy sauce and keep warm.

5 Pour the water out of the wok and return to the heat. Add the remaining groundnut and sesame oils and, when hot, add the garlic, ginger and spring onion and stir-fry for 2 minutes, or until golden. Pour over the fish, garnish with chive leaves and lemon slices and serve immediately with rice and an Oriental salad.

Chinese Five Spice Marinated Salmon

INGREDIENTS

Serves 4

700 g/1½ lb skinless salmon fillet, cut
  into 2.5 cm/1 inch strips
2 medium egg whites
1 tbsp cornflour
vegetable oil for frying
4 spring onions, cut diagonally into
  5 cm/2 inch pieces
125 m/4 fl oz fish stock
lime or lemon wedges, to garnish

For the marinade:

3 tbsp soy sauce
3 tbsp Chinese rice wine or dry sherry
2 tsp sesame oil
1 tbsp soft brown sugar
1 tbsp lime or lemon juice
1 tsp Chinese five spice powder
2–3 dashes hot pepper sauce

1   Combine the marinade ingredients in a shallow, non-metallic baking dish until well blended. Add the salmon strips and stir gently to coat. Leave to marinate in the refrigerator for 20–30 minutes.

2   Using a slotted spoon or fish slice, remove the salmon pieces, drain on absorbent kitchen paper and pat dry. Reserve the marinade.

3   Beat the egg whites with the cornflour to make a batter. Add the salmon strips and stir into the batter until coated completely.

4   Pour enough oil into a large wok to come 5 cm/2 inches up the side and place over a high heat. Working in two or three batches, add the salmon strips and cook for 1–2 minutes or until golden. Remove from the wok with a slotted spoon and drain on absorbent kitchen paper. Reserve.

5   Discard the hot oil and wipe the wok clean. Add the marinade, spring onions and stock to the wok. Bring to the boil and simmer for 1 minute. Add the salmon strips and stir-fry gently until coated in the sauce. Spoon into a warmed, shallow serving dish, garnish with the lime or lemon wedges and serve immediately.

HELPFUL HINT

If you prefer, marinate the salmon for 4–6 hours for a much stronger and more intense flavour.

1

3

4

Stir–fried Tiger Prawns

INGREDIENTS

Serves 4

75 g/3 oz fine egg thread noodles
125 g/4 oz broccoli florets
125 g/4 oz baby sweetcorn, halved
3 tbsp soy sauce
1 tbsp lemon juice
pinch of sugar
1 tsp chilli sauce
1 tsp sesame oil
2 tbsp sunflower oil
450 g/1 lb raw tiger prawns,
  peeled, heads and tails removed,
  and deveined
2.5 cm/1 inch piece fresh root ginger,
  peeled and cut into sticks
1 garlic clove, peeled and chopped
1 red chilli, deseeded and sliced
2 medium eggs, lightly beaten
227 g can water chestnuts, drained
  and sliced

1 Place the noodles in a large bowl, cover with plenty of boiling water and leave to stand for 5 minutes, or according to packet directions, stirring occasionally. Drain and reserve. Blanch the broccoli and sweetcorn in a saucepan of boiling salted water for 2 minutes, then drain and reserve.

2 Meanwhile, mix together the soy sauce, lemon juice, sugar, chilli sauce and sesame oil in a bowl and reserve.

3 Heat a large wok, then add the sunflower oil and heat until just smoking. Add the prawns and stir-fry for 2–3 minutes, or until pink on all sides. Using a slotted spoon, transfer the prawns to a plate and reserve. Add the ginger and stir-fry for 30 seconds. Add the garlic and chilli to the wok and cook for a further 30 seconds.

4 Add the noodles and stir-fry for 3 minutes, until the noodles are crisp. Stir in the prawns, vegetables, eggs and water chestnuts and stir-fry for a further 3 minutes, until the eggs are lightly cooked. Pour over the chilli sauce, stir lightly and serve immediately.

HELPFUL HINT

Egg noodles are available in a variety of thicknesses. All are very quick to cook and are an excellent store-cupboard ingredient.

Coconut Seafood

INGREDIENTS

Serves 4

2 tbsp groundnut oil

450 g/1 lb raw king prawns, peeled

2 bunches spring onions, trimmed
and thickly sliced

1 garlic clove, peeled and chopped

2.5 cm/1 inch piece fresh root ginger,
peeled and cut into matchsticks

125 g/4 oz fresh shiitake mushrooms,
rinsed and halved

150 ml/¼ pint dry white wine

200 ml/7 fl oz carton coconut cream

4 tbsp freshly chopped coriander

salt and freshly ground
black pepper

freshly cooked fragrant Thai rice

1 Heat a large wok, add the oil and heat until it is almost smoking, swirling the oil around the wok to coat the sides. Add the prawns and stir-fry over a high heat for 4–5 minutes, or until browned on all sides. Using a slotted spoon, transfer the prawns to a plate and keep warm in a low oven.

2 Add the spring onions, garlic and ginger to the wok and stir-fry for 1 minute. Add the mushrooms and stir-fry for a further 3 minutes. Using a slotted spoon, transfer the mushroom mixture to a plate and keep warm in a low oven.

3 Add the wine and coconut cream to the wok, bring to the boil and boil rapidly for 4 minutes, until reduced slightly.

4 Return the mushroom mixture and prawns to the wok, bring back to the boil, then simmer for 1 minute, stirring occasionally, until piping hot. Stir in the freshly chopped coriander and season to taste with salt and pepper. Serve immediately with the freshly cooked fragrant Thai rice.

HELPFUL HINT

If coconut cream is not available, grate 50 g/2 oz creamed coconut (see p28) into 175 ml/6 fl oz hot water. Whisk until completely dissolved and use as above.

Prawn Fried Rice

INGREDIENTS

Serves 4

knob of butter

4 medium eggs, beaten

4 tbsp groundnut oil

1 bunch spring onions, trimmed and
finely shredded

125 g/4 oz cooked ham, diced

350 g/12 oz large cooked prawns,
thawed if frozen and peeled

125 g/4 oz peas, thawed if frozen

450 g/1 lb cooked long-grain rice

2 tbsp dark soy sauce

1 tbsp sherry

salt and freshly ground black pepper

1 tbsp freshly shredded coriander

HELPFUL HINT

Use cold cooked rice as it is less likely to stick to the wok. Make sure, however, that the rice is heated right through and is piping hot. Do not re-heat more than once and never keep cooked rice longer than 24 hours.

1 Heat a wok, lightly grease with the butter and when melted, pour in half the beaten eggs. Cook for 4 minutes, stirring frequently, until the egg has set, forming an omelette. Using a fish slice, lift the omelette from the wok and roll up into a sausage shape. When cool, using a sharp knife, slice the omelette into thin rings, then reserve.

2 Wipe the wok clean with absorbent kitchen paper and heat it. Add the oil and heat until just smoking. Add the shredded spring onions, the ham, prawns and peas and stir-fry for 2 minutes, or until heated through thoroughly. Add the cooked rice and stir-fry for a further 2 minutes.

3 Stir in the remaining beaten eggs and stir-fry for 3 minutes, or until the egg has set. Stir in the soy sauce and sherry and season to taste with salt and pepper, then heat until piping hot. Add the omelette rings and gently stir through the mixture, making sure not to break them up. Sprinkle with the freshly shredded coriander and serve immediately.

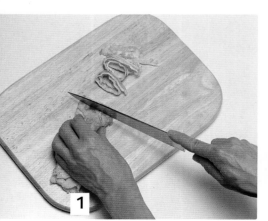

Sweet-&-Sour Rice with Chicken

INGREDIENTS

Serves 4

4 spring onions

2 tsp sesame oil

1 tsp Chinese five spice powder

450 g/1 lb chicken breast,
  cut into cubes

1 tbsp oil

1 garlic clove, peeled and crushed

1 medium onion, peeled and sliced
  into thin wedges

225 g/8 oz long-grain white rice

600 ml/1 pint water

4 tbsp tomato ketchup

1 tbsp tomato purée

2 tbsp honey

1 tbsp vinegar

1 tbsp dark soy sauce

1 carrot, peeled and cut
  into matchsticks

FOOD FACT

Five spice powder is a Chinese seasoning that can be bought in most supermarkets. A mixture of finely ground star anise, fennel, cinnamon, cloves and Szechuan pepper, it adds a unique sweet and spicy aniseed flavour to food.

1 Trim the spring onions, then cut lengthways into fine strips. Drop into a large bowl of iced water and reserve.

2 Mix together the sesame oil and Chinese five spice powder and use to rub into the cubed chicken. Heat the wok, then add the oil and, when hot, cook the garlic and onion for 2–3 minutes, or until transparent and softened.

3 Add the chicken and stir-fry over a medium-high heat until the chicken is golden and cooked through. Using a slotted spoon, remove from the wok and keep warm.

4 Stir the rice into the wok and add the water, tomato ketchup, tomato purée, honey, vinegar and soy sauce. Stir well to mix. Bring to the boil, then simmer until almost all of the liquid is absorbed. Stir in the carrot and reserved chicken and continue to cook for 3–4 minutes.

5 Drain the spring onions, which will have become curly. Garnish with the spring onion curls and serve immediately with the rice and chicken.

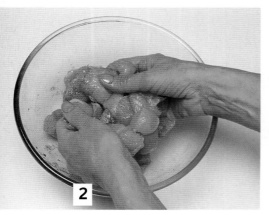

2

3

4

Special Fried Rice

INGREDIENTS

Serves 4

1 large egg
1 tsp sesame oil
350 g/8 oz long-grain white rice
1 tbsp groundnut oil
450 g/1 lb boneless, skinless
    chicken breast, diced
8 spring onions, trimmed and sliced
2 large carrots, trimmed and cut
    into matchsticks
125 g/4 oz sugar snap peas
125 g/4 oz raw tiger prawns, peeled
2 tsp Chinese five spice powder
1 tbsp soy sauce
1 tbsp Thai fish sauce
1 tbsp rice wine vinegar

FOOD FACT

A classic of Chinese ingredients, sesame oil is richly coloured and strongly flavoured. It has a low smoking temperature, so should not be heated to an extremely high heat, otherwise the delicious sesame flavour will be lost.

1   Beat the egg in a bowl with ½ teaspoon of the sesame oil and 2 teaspoons of water. Heat a frying pan over a medium-high heat and swirl in 2 tablespoons of the egg mixture to form a paper-thin omelette. Remove and reserve. Repeat this process until all the egg has been used.

2   Cook the rice in lightly salted boiling water for 12 minutes, or until tender. Drain and reserve.

3   Heat a wok, then add the remaining sesame oil with the groundnut oil and stir-fry the chicken for 5 minutes until cooked through. Using a slotted spoon, remove from the wok and keep warm.

4   Add the spring onions, carrot and sugar snap peas to the wok and stir-fry for 2–3 minutes. Add the prawns and stir-fry for 2–3 minutes, or until pink. Return the chicken to the wok with the Chinese five spice powder and stir-fry for 1 minute. Stir in the drained rice.

5   Mix together the soy sauce, fish sauce and vinegar. Pour into the wok and continue to stir-fry for 2–3 minutes. Roll the papery omelettes into tight rolls and slice to form thin strips. Stir into the rice and serve immediately.

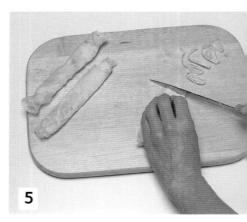

Chicken Satay Salad

INGREDIENTS

Serves 4

4 tbsp crunchy peanut butter

1 tbsp chilli sauce

1 garlic clove, peeled and crushed

2 tbsp cider vinegar

2 tbsp light soy sauce

2 tbsp dark soy sauce

2 tsp soft brown sugar

pinch of salt

2 tsp freshly ground Szechuan
    peppercorns

450 g/1 lb dried egg noodles

2 tbsp sesame oil

1 tbsp groundnut oil

450 g/1 lb skinless, boneless chicken
    breast fillets, cut into cubes

shredded celery leaves, to garnish

cos lettuce, to serve

FOOD FACT

Szechuan peppercorns are the dried berries of a shrub that is a member of the citrus family. The smell is reminiscent of lavender and they have a sharp, mildly spicy flavour. They are often toasted in a dry frying pan before grinding, to bring out their distinctive flavour.

1 Place the peanut butter, chilli sauce, garlic, cider vinegar, soy sauces, sugar, salt and ground peppercorns in a food processor and blend to form a smooth paste. Scrape into a bowl, cover and chill in the refrigerator until required.

2 Bring a large saucepan of lightly salted water to the boil. Add the noodles and cook for 3–5 minutes. Drain and plunge into cold water. Drain again and toss in the sesame oil. Leave to cool.

3 Heat the wok until very hot, add the oil and, when hot, add the chicken cubes. Stir-fry for 5–6 minutes until the chicken is golden brown and cooked through.

4 Remove the chicken from the wok using a slotted spoon and add to the noodles, together with the peanut sauce. Mix lightly together, then sprinkle with the shredded celery leaves and either serve immediately or leave until cold, then serve with cos lettuce.

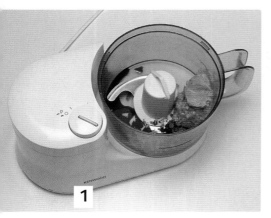
1

2

3

Chicken & Baby Vegetable Stir Fry

INGREDIENTS

Serves 4

2 tbsp groundnut oil

1 small red chilli, deseeded and
finely chopped

150 g/5 oz chicken breast
or thigh meat, skinned and
cut into cubes

2 baby leeks, trimmed and sliced

12 asparagus spears, halved

125 g/4 oz mangetout, trimmed

125 g/4 oz baby carrots, trimmed and
halved lengthways

125 g/4 oz fine green beans, trimmed
and diagonally sliced

125 g/4 oz baby sweetcorn,
diagonally halved

50 ml/2 fl oz chicken stock

2 tsp light soy sauce

1 tbsp dry sherry

1 tsp sesame oil

toasted sesame seeds, to garnish

HELPFUL HINT

Look out for packs of mixed baby
vegetables in the supermarket.
They are often available ready-
trimmed and will save a lot of time.

1 Heat the wok until very hot and add the oil. Add the chopped chilli
and chicken and stir-fry for 4–5 minutes, or until the chicken is
cooked and golden.

2 Increase the heat, add the leeks to the chicken and stir-fry for 2
minutes. Add the asparagus spears, mangetout peas, baby carrots,
green beans, and baby sweetcorn. Stir-fry for 3–4 minutes, or until
the vegetables soften slightly but still retain a slight crispness.

3 In a small bowl, mix together the chicken stock, soy sauce,
dry sherry and sesame oil. Pour into the wok, stir and cook
until heated through. Sprinkle with the toasted sesame seeds
and serve immediately.

Stir-fried Chicken with Basil

INGREDIENTS

Serves 4

3 tbsp sunflower oil

3 tbsp green curry paste

450 g/1 lb skinless, boneless
  chicken breast fillets, trimmed
  and cut into cubes

8 cherry tomatoes

100 ml/4 fl oz coconut cream

2 tbsp soft brown sugar

2 tbsp Thai fish sauce

1 red chilli, deseeded and thinly sliced

1 green chilli, deseeded and
  thinly sliced

75 g/3 oz fresh torn basil leaves

sprigs of fresh coriander, to garnish

freshly steamed white rice, to serve

FOOD FACT

Creamed coconut is common-place in Eastern cooking. It usually comes in the form of a waxy block of hardened coconut cream. It is very high in fat, but adds a gorgeous, rich creaminess to dishes. It can be chopped or grated and melts very easily on contact with the hot sauce.

1 Heat the wok, then add the oil and heat for 1 minute. Add the green curry paste and cook, stirring for 1 minute to release the flavour and cook the paste. Add the chicken and stir-fry over a high heat for 2 minutes, making sure the chicken is coated thoroughly with the green curry paste.

2 Reduce the heat under the wok, then add the cherry tomatoes and cook, stirring gently, for 2–3 minutes, or until the tomatoes burst and begin to disintegrate into the green curry paste.

3 Add half the coconut cream to the wok along with the brown sugar, Thai fish sauce and the red and green chillies. Stir-fry gently for 5 minutes, or until the sauce is amalgamated and the chicken is thoroughly cooked.

4 Just before serving, sprinkle the chicken with the torn basil leaves and add the remaining coconut cream, then serve immediately with freshly steamed white rice garnished with fresh coriander sprigs.

Szechuan Turkey Noodles

INGREDIENTS

Serves 4

1 tbsp tomato paste

2 tsp black bean sauce

2 tsp cider vinegar

salt and freshly ground black pepper

½ tsp Szechuan pepper

2 tsp sugar

4 tsp sesame oil

225 g/8 oz dried egg noodles

2 tbsp groundnut oil

2 tsp freshly grated root ginger

3 garlic cloves, peeled and
  roughly chopped

2 shallots, peeled and finely chopped

2 courgettes, trimmed and cut into
  fine matchsticks

450 g/1 lb turkey breast, skinned and
  cut into strips

deep-fried onion rings, to garnish

FOOD FACT

Fresh ginger is indispensable as a flavouring in Chinese cookery. Its pungent, spicy, fresh taste adds a subtle but very distinctive flavour to all types of dishes. When buying root ginger, look for firm pieces with no signs of shrivelling.

1 Mix together the tomato paste, black bean sauce, cider vinegar, a pinch of salt and pepper, the sugar and half the sesame oil. Chill in the refrigerator for 30 minutes.

2 Bring a large saucepan of lightly salted water to the boil and add the noodles. Cook for 3–5 minutes, drain and plunge immediately into cold water. Toss with the remaining sesame oil and reserve.

3 Heat the wok until very hot, then add the oil and when hot, add the ginger, garlic and shallots. Stir-fry for 20 seconds, then add the courgettes and turkey strips. Stir-fry for 3–4 minutes, or until the turkey strips are sealed.

4 Add the prepared chilled black bean sauce and continue to stir-fry for another 4 minutes over a high heat. Add the drained noodles to the wok and stir until the noodles, turkey, vegetables and the sauce are well mixed together. Garnish with the deep-fried onion rings and serve immediately.

1

3

4

Sweet-&-Sour Turkey

INGREDIENTS

Serves 4

2 tbsp groundnut oil

2 garlic cloves, peeled and chopped

1 tbsp freshly grated root ginger

4 spring onions, trimmed and cut
into 4 cm/1½ inch lengths

450 g/1 lb turkey breast, skinned and
cut into strips

1 red pepper, deseeded and cut into
2.5 cm/1 inch squares

225 g/8 oz canned water chestnuts,
drained

150 ml/¼ pint chicken stock

2 tbsp Chinese rice wine

3 tbsp light soy sauce

2 tsp dark soy sauce

2 tbsp tomato paste

2 tbsp white wine vinegar

1 tbsp sugar

1 tbsp cornflour

egg-fried rice, to serve

TASTY TIP

To make egg-fried rice, stir-fry
450 g/1 lb cold cooked rice with 2
beaten eggs until the eggs have set.

1   Heat the wok over a high heat, add the oil and when hot, add the
garlic, ginger and spring onions, stir-fry for 20 seconds.

2   Add the turkey to the wok and stir-fry for 2 minutes, or until
beginning to colour. Add the peppers and water chestnuts and
stir-fry for a further 2 minutes.

3   Mix the chicken stock, Chinese rice wine, light and dark soy sauce,
tomato paste, white wine vinegar and the sugar together in a small
jug or bowl. Add the mixture to the wok, stir and bring the sauce to
the boil.

4   Mix together the cornflour with 2 tablespoons of water and add to
the wok. Reduce the heat and simmer for 3 minutes, or until the
turkey is cooked thoroughly and the sauce slightly thickened and
glossy. Serve immediately with egg-fried rice.

Fried Ginger Rice with Soy Glazed Duck

INGREDIENTS

Serves 4-6

2 duck breasts, skinned and
diagonally cut into thin slices

2–3 tbsp Japanese soy sauce

1 tbsp mirin (sweet rice wine)
or sherry

2 tbsp brown sugar

5 cm/2 inch piece of fresh root ginger,
peeled and finely chopped

4 tbsp peanut or vegetable oil

2 garlic cloves, peeled and crushed

300 g/11 oz long-grain brown rice

900 ml/1½ pints chicken stock

freshly ground black pepper

125 g/4 oz lean ham, diced

175 g/6 oz mangetout, diagonally cut
in half

8 spring onions, trimmed and
diagonally thinly sliced

1 tbsp freshly chopped coriander

sweet or hot chilli sauce, to taste
(optional)

sprigs of fresh coriander, to garnish

1   Put the duck slices in a bowl with 1 tablespoon of the soy sauce, the mirin, 1 teaspoon of the sugar and one-third of the ginger; stir. Leave to stand.

2   Heat 2 tablespoons of the oil in a large heavy-based saucepan. Add the garlic and half the remaining ginger and stir-fry for 1 minute. Add the rice and cook for 3 minutes, stirring constantly, until translucent.

3   Stir in all but 125 ml/4 fl oz of the stock, with 1 teaspoon of the soy sauce, and bring to the boil. Season with pepper. Reduce the heat to very low and simmer, covered, for 25–30 minutes until the rice is tender and the liquid is absorbed. Cover and leave to stand.

4   Heat the remaining oil in a large frying pan or wok. Drain the duck strips and add to the frying pan. Stir-fry for 2–3 minutes until just coloured. Add 1 tablespoon of soy sauce and the remaining sugar and cook for 1 minute until glazed. Transfer to a plate and keep warm.

5   Stir in the ham, mangetout, spring onions, the remaining ginger and the chopped coriander. Add the remaining stock and duck marinade and cook until the liquid is almost reduced. Fork in the rice and a little chilli sauce to taste (if using); stir well. Turn into a serving dish and top with the duck. Garnish with coriander sprigs and serve immediately.

Duck in Black Bean Sauce

INGREDIENTS

Serves 4

450 g/1 lb duck breast, skinned
1 tbsp light soy sauce
1 tbsp Chinese rice wine or dry sherry
2.5 cm/1 inch piece fresh root ginger
3 garlic cloves
2 spring onions
2 tbsp Chinese preserved black beans
1 tbsp groundnut or vegetable oil
150 ml/¼ pint chicken stock
shredded spring onions, to garnish
freshly cooked noodles, to serve

HELPFUL HINT

The way in which a dish is presented and garnished is extremely important in both Chinese and Thai cuisine. Fine shreds of colourful vegetables are simple to make. For spring onion shreds, cut off most of the white bulb end and trim the tops. Cut the remaining green part lengthways into fine shreds. These can be curled by dropping them into iced water for a few minutes.

1 Using a sharp knife, trim the duck breasts, removing any fat. Slice thickly and place in a shallow dish. Mix together the soy sauce and Chinese rice wine or sherry and pour over the duck. Leave to marinate for 1 hour in the refrigerator, then drain and discard the marinade.

2 Peel the ginger and chop finely. Peel the garlic cloves and either chop finely or crush. Trim the root from the spring onions, discard the outer leaves and chop. Finely chop the black beans.

3 Heat a wok or large frying pan, add the oil and when very hot, add the ginger, garlic, spring onions and black beans and stir-fry for 30 seconds. Add the drained duck and stir-fry for 3–5 minutes or until the duck is browned.

4 Add the chicken stock to the wok, bring to the boil, then reduce the heat and simmer for 5 minutes, or until the duck is cooked and the sauce is reduced and thickened. Remove from the heat. Tip on to a bed of freshly cooked noodles, garnish with spring onion shreds and serve immediately.

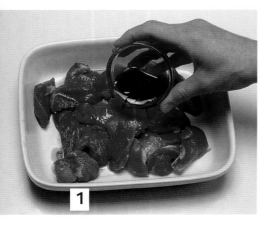

1

3

4

Crispy Roast Duck Legs with Pancakes

INGREDIENTS

Serves 6

900 g/2 lb plums, halved
25 g/1 oz butter
2 star anise
1 tsp freshly grated root ginger
50 g/2 oz soft brown sugar
zest and juice of 1 orange
salt and freshly ground black pepper
4 duck legs
3 tbsp dark soy sauce
2 tbsp dark brown sugar
½ cucumber, cut into matchsticks
1 small bunch spring onions,
   trimmed and shredded
18 ready-made Chinese
   pancakes, warmed

1 Preheat the oven to 220°C/425°F/Gas Mark 7, 15 minutes before cooking. Discard the stones from the plums and place in a saucepan with the butter, star anise, ginger, brown sugar and orange zest and juice. Season to taste with pepper. Cook over a gentle heat until the sugar has dissolved. Bring to the boil, then reduce heat and simmer for 15 minutes, stirring occasionally until the plums are soft and the mixture is thick. Remove the star anise. Leave to cool.

2 Using a fork, prick the duck legs all over. Place in a large bowl and pour boiling water over to remove some of the fat. Drain, pat dry on absorbent kitchen paper and leave until cold.

3 Mix together the soy sauce, dark brown sugar and the ½ teaspoon of salt. Rub this mixture generously over the duck legs. Transfer to a wire rack set over a roasting tin and roast in the preheated oven for 30–40 minutes, or until well cooked and the skin is browned and crisp. Remove from the oven and leave to rest for 10 minutes.

4 Shred the duck meat using a fork to hold the hot duck leg and another to remove the meat. Transfer to a warmed serving platter with the cucumber and spring onions. Serve immediately with the plum compote and warmed pancakes.

TASTY TIP

Warm the pancakes by stacking and wrapping in tinfoil and placing on a plate in a steamer – or for 15 minutes in the oven, after removing the duck and turning the oven off.

2

1

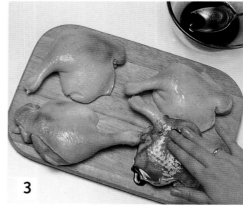

3

Chinese Beef with Angel Hair Pasta

INGREDIENTS

Serves 4

1 tbsp pink peppercorns
1 tbsp chilli powder
1 tbsp Szechuan pepper
3 tbsp light soy sauce
3 tbsp dry sherry
450 g/1 lb sirloin steak, cut into strips
350 g/12 oz angel hair pasta
1 tbsp sesame oil
1 tbsp sunflower oil
1 bunch spring onions, trimmed
   and finely shredded, plus extra
   to garnish
1 red pepper, deseeded and
   thinly sliced
1 green pepper, deseeded and
   thinly sliced
1 tbsp toasted sesame seeds,
   to garnish

1 Crush the peppercorns, using a pestle and mortar. Transfer to a shallow bowl and combine with the chilli powder, Szechuan pepper, light soy sauce and sherry. Add the beef strips and stir until lightly coated. Cover and place in the refrigerator to marinate for 3 hours; stir occasionally during this time.

2 When ready to cook, bring a large pan of lightly salted water to a rolling boil. Add the pasta and cook according to the packet instructions, or until 'al dente'. Drain thoroughly and return to the pan. Add the sesame oil and toss lightly. Keep the pasta warm.

3 Heat a wok or large frying pan, add the sunflower oil and heat until very hot. Add the shredded spring onions with the sliced red and green peppers and stir-fry for 2 minutes.

4 Drain the beef, reserving the marinade, then add the beef to the wok or pan and stir-fry for 3 minutes. Pour the marinade and stir-fry for 1–2 minutes, until the steak is tender.

5 Pile the pasta on to four warmed plates. Top with the stir-fried beef and peppers and garnish with toasted sesame seeds and shredded spring onions. Serve immediately.

1

3

4

Coconut Beef

INGREDIENTS

Serves 4

450 g/1 lb beef rump or sirloin steak
4 tbsp groundnut oil
2 bunches spring onions, trimmed
  and thickly sliced
1 red chilli, deseeded and chopped
1 garlic clove, peeled and chopped
2 cm/1 inch piece fresh root ginger,
  peeled and cut into matchsticks
125 g/4 oz shiitake mushrooms
200 ml/7 fl oz coconut cream
150 ml/¼ pint chicken stock
4 tbsp freshly chopped coriander
salt and freshly ground black pepper
freshly cooked rice, to serve

FOOD FACT

Shiitake mushrooms, which grow naturally on decaying trees, are now cultivated on the shii tree, hence their name. Here they are used fresh, but are often used dried. To prepare fresh mushrooms, wipe with damp absorbent kitchen paper, remove and discard the tough stalks and slice the caps, if large.

1 Trim off any fat or gristle from the beef and cut into thin strips. Heat a wok or large frying pan, add 2 tablespoons of the oil and heat until just smoking. Add the beef and cook for 5–8 minutes, turning occasionally, until browned on all sides. Using a slotted spoon, transfer the beef to a plate and keep warm.

2 Add the remaining oil to the wok and heat until almost smoking. Add the spring onions, chilli, garlic and ginger and cook for 1 minute, stirring occasionally. Add the mushrooms and stir-fry for 3 minutes. Using a slotted spoon, transfer the mushroom mixture to a plate and keep warm.

3 Return the beef to the wok, pour in the coconut cream and stock. Bring to the boil and simmer for 3–4 minutes, or until the juices are slightly reduced and the beef is just tender.

4 Return the mushroom mixture to the wok and heat through. Stir in the chopped coriander and season to taste with salt and pepper. Serve immediately with freshly cooked rice.

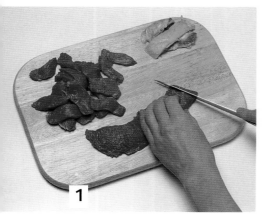
1

2

3

Chilli Beef

INGREDIENTS

Serves 4

550 g/1¼ lb beef rump steak
2 tbsp groundnut oil
2 carrots, peeled and cut
  into matchsticks
125 g/4 oz mangetout, shredded
125 g/4 oz beansprouts
1 green chilli, deseeded and chopped
2 tbsp sesame seeds
freshly cooked rice, to serve

For the marinade:

1 garlic clove, peeled and chopped
3 tbsp soy sauce
1 tbsp sweet chilli sauce
4 tbsp groundnut oil

FOOD FACT

Chillies have become a favourite Chinese ingredient, especially in Szechuan cooking. Chilli sauce is a mixture of crushed fresh chillies, plums, vinegar and salt. It is available in several varieties: extra hot, hot or sweet (see p48), as used here, which is the mildest version. Chilli sauce may be used as a marinade or as a dip.

1 Using a sharp knife, trim the beef, discarding any fat or gristle, then cut into thin strips and reserve. Combine all the marinade ingredients in a bowl and add the beef. Turn the beef in the marinade until coated evenly, cover with clingfilm and leave to marinate in the refrigerator for at least 30 minutes.

2 Heat a wok or large frying pan, add the groundnut oil and heat until almost smoking, then add the carrots and stir-fry for 3–4 minutes, or until softened. Add the mangetout and stir-fry for a further 1 minute. Using a slotted spoon, transfer the vegetables to a plate and keep warm.

3 Lift the beef strips from the marinade, shaking to remove excess marinade. Reserve the marinade. Add the beef to the wok and stir-fry for 3 minutes or until browned all over.

4 Return the stir-fried vegetables to the wok together with the beansprouts, chilli and sesame seeds and cook for 1 minute. Stir in the reserved marinade and stir-fry for 1–2 minutes or until heated through. Tip into a warmed serving dish or spoon on to individual plates and serve immediately with freshly cooked rice.

Beef & Baby Corn Stir Fry

INGREDIENTS

Serves 4

3 tbsp light soy sauce

1 tbsp clear honey, warmed

450 g/1 lb beef rump steak,
  trimmed and thinly sliced

6 tbsp groundnut oil

125 g/4 oz shiitake mushrooms,
  wiped and halved

125 g/4 oz beansprouts, rinsed

2.5 cm/1 inch piece fresh root ginger,
  peeled and cut into matchsticks

125 g/4 oz mangetout,
  halved lengthways

125 g/4 oz broccoli, trimmed
  and cut into florets

1 medium carrot, peeled and
  cut into matchsticks

125 g/4 oz baby sweetcorn cobs,
  halved lengthways

¼ head Chinese leaves, shredded

1 tbsp chilli sauce

3 tbsp black bean sauce

1 tbsp dry sherry

freshly cooked noodles, to serve

1 Mix together the soy sauce and honey in a shallow dish. Add the sliced beef and turn to coat evenly. Cover with clingfilm and leave to marinate for at least 30 minutes, turning occasionally.

2 Heat a wok or large frying pan, add 2 tablespoons of the oil and heat until just smoking. Add the mushrooms and stir-fry for 1 minute. Add the bean sprouts and stir-fry for 1 minute. Using a slotted spoon, transfer the mushroom mixture to a plate and keep warm.

3 Drain the beef, reserving the marinade. Reheat the wok, pour in 2 tablespoons of the oil and heat until smoking. Add the beef and stir-fry for 4 minutes or until browned. Transfer to a plate and keep warm.

4 Add the remaining oil to the wok and heat until just smoking. Add the ginger, mangetout, broccoli, carrot and the baby sweetcorn with the shredded Chinese leaves and stir-fry for 3 minutes. Stir in the chilli and black bean sauces, the sherry, the reserved marinade and the beef and mushroom mixture. Stir-fry for 2 minutes, then serve immediately with freshly cooked noodles.

Step-by-Step, Practical Recipes Chinese: Tips & Hints

Food Fact

The meat recipes in this book focus on beef, but pork is the most popular meat of China. In rural parts, nearly every family will keep a pig, which thrives on kitchen scraps. Belly of pork, also known as streaky pork, is a thin cut of meat with roughly the same proportion of fat to lean meat in thin alternate layers. In Chinese cooking, it is usually well cooked so that the meat is tender and the fat golden brown and crispy.

Tasty Tip

For a simple vegetable accompaniment that can be served with other dishes, heat a wok until really hot, then add 1 tablespoon of oil. Add 1 chopped garlic clove and a little grated ginger, a finely sliced red, green and yellow pepper, some mangetout and spring onion. Stir-fry for 3–4 minutes and serve.

Helpful Hint

Before cooking any meat, pork or beef, that has been marinated beforehand, shake off as much marinade as possible, then pat the meat dry with absorbent kitchen paper. This will ensure that the meat is fried in the hot oil and browns properly. If too much liquid is added with the meat, it tends to steam in the juices.

Helpful Hint

For a really easy, classic Chinese dipping sauce, blend together 2 tablespoons dark soy sauce, 1 tablespoon Chinese rice wine or dry sherry, 2 teaspoons chilli bean sauce, 2 teaspoons toasted sesame seed oil and 1 teaspoon caster sugar. Stir in one very finely chopped spring onion.

Food Fact

Chinese leaves have a delicate, mild cabbage-like flavour and are often used in Chinese stir-fries, or steamed lightly and served as a vegetable side dish. They have pale, tightly wrapped crinkly leaves and crisp white stems. Because they are now grown in and imported from Spain, Holland and Israel, they are available all year round. They will keep for at least a week in the salad drawer of your refrigerator.

Tasty Tip

Chinese spareribs are another Chinese classic and taste best if they are placed in a marinade overnight. This not only brings out the flavour of meat, but makes it wonderfully tender as well. If you do not have enough time for this, place the ribs in a saucepan and pour in enough water to just cover. Add 1 tablespoon of wine vinegar, bring to the boil, then simmer gently for 15 minutes. Drain well, coat in the marinade, and roast straight away, basting occasionally.

Helpful Hint

As well as the more exotic spices listed in this book, one of the most commonly used seasonings in Chinese dishes is garlic. Choose firm garlic, preferably with a pinkish tinge and store in a cool dry place.

Food Fact

As well as shiitake mushroom (see p42), oyster mushrooms are also often used in Chinese cooking. They are prized for their subtle flavour and delicate, almost slippery texture. Originally from the East, they are now widely available.

Food Fact

Dried flat rice noodles, rice sticks and stir-fry rice noodles are all made from rice flour and come in varying thicknesses. Check on the packet for cooking instructions; they usually need to be soaked only briefly in boiling water, about 2–3 minutes, or slightly longer in hot water.

Helpful Hint

It is tempting to assume that sweet chilli sauce (see p44) is not hot, but it can still have a good chilli kick. It is wise to adjust the quantity according to taste.

Food Fact

Yellow bean sauce is a thick, spicy sauce made with yellow beans, flour and salt fermented together. It is one of many ready-made sauces commonly used in Chinese cookery. It is quite salty but adds a distinctive flavour. Available as whole beans in a thick sauce or as mashed beans (also known as crushed bean sauce), the whole bean sauce tends to be less salty. Yellow bean sauce is available from either large supermarkets or Asian grocers. Black bean sauce is sometimes substituted.

First published in 2012 by
FLAME TREE PUBLISHING LTD
Crabtree Hall, Crabtree Lane, Fulham,
London, SW6 6TY, United Kingdom
www.flametreepublishing.com

NOTE: Recipes using uncooked eggs should be avoided by infants, the elderly, pregnant women and anyone suffering from an illness.

18 17 16 15 14 13 12   10 9 8 7 6 5 4 3 2 1

ISBN: 978-0-85775-615-2

ACKNOWLEDGEMENTS: Authors: Catherine Atkinson, Juliet Barker, Gina Steer, Vicki Smallwood, Carol Tennant, Mari Mererid Williams, Elizabeth Wolf-Cohen and Simone Wright. Photography: Colin Bowling, Paul Forrester and Stephen Brayne. Home Economists and Stylists: Jacqueline Bellefontaine, Mandy Phipps, Vicki Smallwood and Penny Stephens. All props supplied by Barbara Stewart at Surfaces. Publisher and Creative Director: Nick Wells. Editorial: Catherine Taylor, Sarah Goulding, Marcus Hardie, Gina Steer and Karen Fitzpatrick. Design and Production: Chris Herbert, Mike Spender, Colin Rudderham and Helen Wall.